NEW ROUTES TO ENGLISH

STUDENT BOOK ONE

Senior Author
Gloria Paulik Sampson

Collier Macmillan International, Inc.
New York
Collier Macmillan Publishers
London

STAFF

NEW ROUTES TO ENGLISH

PROJECT EDITOR: Judith Reeves-Stevens
DESIGN AND ART DIRECTION: William Fox Associates
SENIOR EDITOR: Elma Schemenauer

Student Book One

ARTISTS

Ruth Bagshaw–pages 43, 102, 103, 118, 119, 121, 122, 123, 124.
Alan and Lea Daniel in collaboration with J. Merle Smith–pages
15, 16, 17, 18, 19, 22, 30, 32, 33, 34, 35, 36, 37, 38, 39, 40, 41, 58,
59, 60, 61, 62, 63, 64, 65, 66, 67, 70, 71, 74, 75, 76, 77, 80, 81, 86,
87, 88, 89, 90, 91, 94, 95, 116, 117.
Helen Fox–pages 10, 11, 14, 15, 24, 25, 26, 27, 28, 29, 104, 105, 106,
107, 108, 109, 110, 111, 112, 113, 114, 115.
Jack Gray–pages 12, 68, 69, 72, 73, 78, 79, 82, 83, 84, 85.
Vladyana Krykorka–pages 54, 55, 92, 93, 96, 97, 98, 99.
John Mardon–pages 5, 6, 7, 8, 9.
Louise Wiatrowski–pages 42, 44, 45, 46, 47, 48, 49, 50, 51, 52,
53, 56, 57.

ACKNOWLEDGMENTS

"Sheep should not. ..." and "How many cans can a canner can?" from *A Twister of Twists, A Tangler of Tongues* by Alvin Schwartz. Copyright © 1972 by Alvin Schwartz. Reprinted by permission of J. B. Lippincott Company and Andre Deutsch Limited.

"Sit Down, Sister" from *More Songs to Grow On* by Beatrice Landeck, arrangement by Florence White. © Copyrighted: Edward B. Marks Music Corporation. Used by permission.

"Song of the Train" from *Mr. Bidery's Garden* by David McCord. Copyright 1952 by David McCord. Reprinted by permission of David McCord, Harrap and Company Limited, and Little Brown and Co.

"Theophilus, the Thistle Sifter" from *A Rocket in My Pocket,* compiled by Carl Withers.
Copyright 1948 by Carl Withers. Copyright © 1976 by Samuel H. Halperin. Reprinted by permission of The Bodley Head and Holt, Rinehart and Winston, Publishers.

10 9 8 7 6 5 4 3

ISBN-0-02-975780-0
Library of Congress Catalog Card Number: 79-54777

Collier Macmillan International, Inc.
866 Third Avenue, New York, N.Y. 10022

Collier Macmillan Canada, Ltd.

Printed in the United States of America

Table of Contents

unit one

What are you doing?

We are walking.

Are we walking? Yes, we are.

Are we standing up? Yes, we are.

We are sitting down.

We are standing up.

Are we walking?   No, we are not.*
We are sitting down.

Are we standing up?   No, we are not.
We are sitting down.

* are not OR aren't

What are you doing?

I am getting a book.

I am opening a book.

I am closing a book.

I am holding a pencil.

I am opening a window.

I am closing a window.

I am opening a door.

What are you doing?

I am picking up the box.

I am putting down the box.

I am opening the box.

I am closing the box.

Are you opening the door?

Yes, I am.

Are you getting a book?

Yes, I am.

Are you picking up a pencil?

No, I am not.
I am picking up a book.

Are you opening the box?

No, I am not.
I am closing the box.

What is she doing?

She is catching the ball.

She is hitting the ball.

She is throwing the ball.

She is bouncing the ball.

Is she bouncing the ball?
Yes, she is.

She is jumping up.

She is hitting the ball.

Is she jumping up?
No, she is not.*
She is hitting the ball.

*is not OR isn't

What is he doing?

He is kicking the ball.

He is running.

Is he running?
Yes, he is.

He is falling down.

He is getting up.

He is hitting the ball.

Is he kicking the ball?
No, he is not.
He is hitting the ball.

What is he doing?   What is she doing?

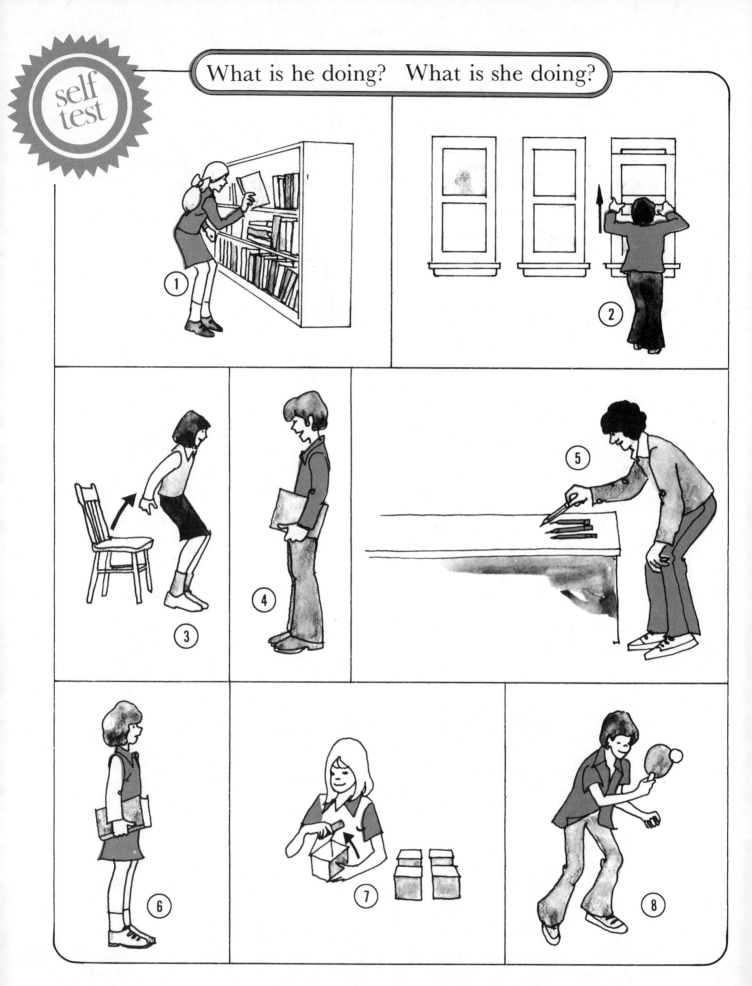

unit two

PRONUNCIATION

Freddy's feet feel frigid.

Violet's vine violates gravity.

Sam's shirt seems short.

Lizzy's nose looks like a rose.

This is my body.

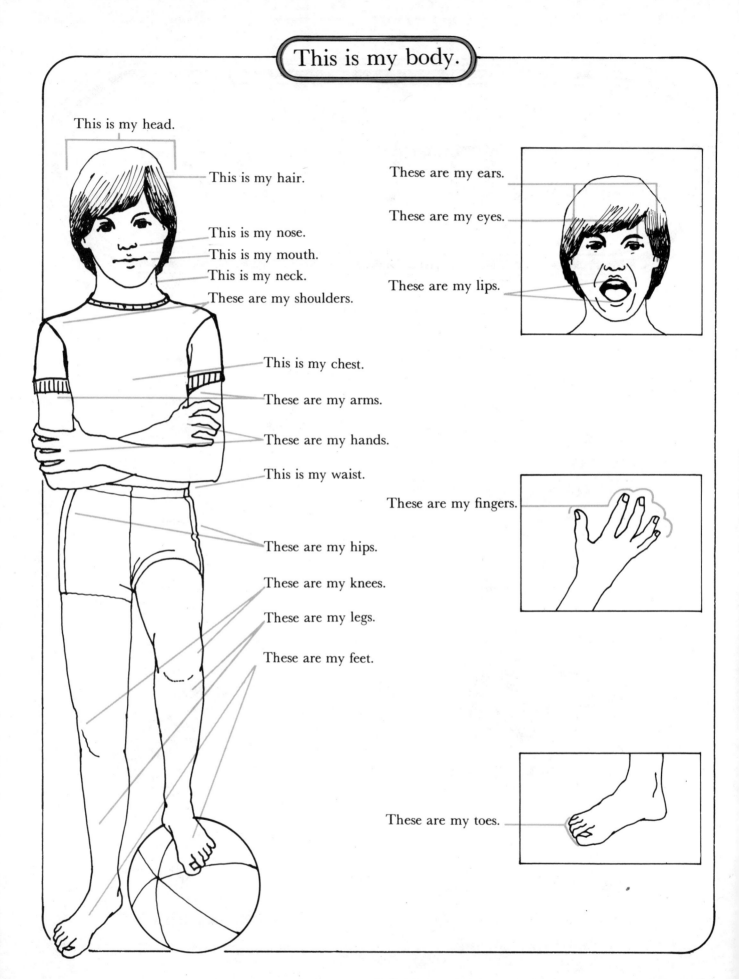

This is my head.

This is my hair.

This is my nose.
This is my mouth.
This is my neck.
These are my shoulders.

This is my chest.

These are my arms.

These are my hands.

This is my waist.

These are my hips.

These are my knees.

These are my legs.

These are my feet.

These are my ears.

These are my eyes.

These are my lips.

These are my fingers.

These are my toes.

What is your name?

My name is Rose Lanski.

What is her name?

Her name is Rose Lanski.

What is his name?

His name is Bob MacMillan.

Whose clothes are these?

Bonnie

Kate

Leo

Bob

Rose

Whose socks are these?

These are Leo's socks.
They are his socks.

Whose stockings are these?

These are Kate's stockings.
They are her stockings.

Whose pants are these?

These are Bob's pants.
They are his pants.

Whose shoes are these?

These are Rose's shoes.
They are her shoes.

Whose jacket is this? This is Leo's jacket. It is his jacket.	Whose dress is this? This is Kate's dress. It is her dress.
Whose shirt is this? This is Bob's shirt. It is his shirt.	Whose purse is this? This is Rose's purse. It is her purse.
Whose belt is this? This is Bob's belt. It is his belt.	Whose blouse is this? This is Rose's blouse. It is her blouse.

Whose clothes are those?

Whose coat is that? That is Kate's coat. It is her coat.	
Whose underwear is that? That is Bob's underwear. It is his underwear.	
Whose jeans are those? Those are Bonnie's jeans. They are her jeans.	
Whose sweater is that? That is Rose's sweater. It is her sweater.	
Whose skirt is that? That is Rose's skirt. It is her skirt.	
Whose shoe is that? That is Leo's shoe. It is his shoe.	

Is this Leo's shirt? No, it is not.	Is that Leo's shirt? Yes, it is.
Are these Kate's shoes? No, they are not.	Are those Kate's shoes? Yes, they are.

Whose clothes are those?

Those are Bob's and Leo's clothes. OR
Those are their shirts.
Those are their socks.

Whose clothes are those?

Those are our clothes. OR
Those are our shirts.
Those are our socks.

Kate

Rose

Leo

Bob

What are they doing?

1. Lee and Len are sleeping.

2. They are waking up.

3. They are washing their faces.

4. They are brushing their teeth.

5. They are taking off their pajamas.

6. They are combing their hair.

7. They are sitting down.

8. They are eating breakfast.

9. They are clearing the table.

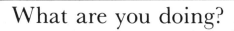

What are you doing?

What are you doing?

    We are putting on our shoes.

Are you putting on your shoes?

    Yes, we are.

What are you doing?

    We are clearing our desks.

Are you getting your pencils?

    No, we are not.
    We are clearing our desks.

unit three

A

B	I	N	G	O
7	3	2	12	17
4	8	●	20	14
1	6	11	13	19
5	9	15	18	16

B

B	I	N	G	O
9	1	6	16	14
5	4	●	20	11
3	8	10	17	18
7	2	15	13	12

C

B	I	N	G	O
5	4	8	17	14
2	6	●	20	18
7	3	12	15	13
10	9	16	11	19

D

B	I	N	G	O
8	4	9	13	18
1	7	●	19	16
5	3	10	12	14
2	6	17	15	11

Where is it?   Where are they?

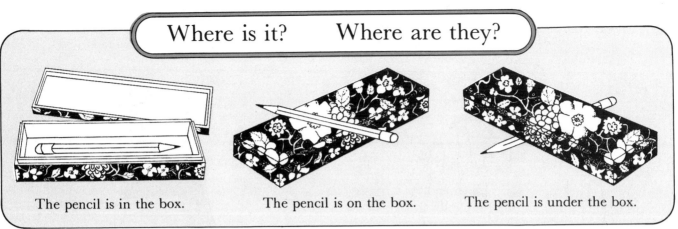

The pencil is in the box.   The pencil is on the box.   The pencil is under the box.

Where is my pencil?   It is in your pocket.

Where is my book?   It is on your desk.

Where are my shoes?   They are under your desk.

The boy's jacket is on a hook.
His glasses are on his nose.
His hands are on his hips.
His socks are on his feet.
His shoes are on his feet.
He is standing on the floor.

Her glasses are on her nose.
Her book is in her hands.
She is sitting in a chair.

She is sitting on a chair.

self test

1. What are they doing?

2. Where are they sitting?

3. Where are their feet?

4. Where are their books?

5. Where are their pencils?

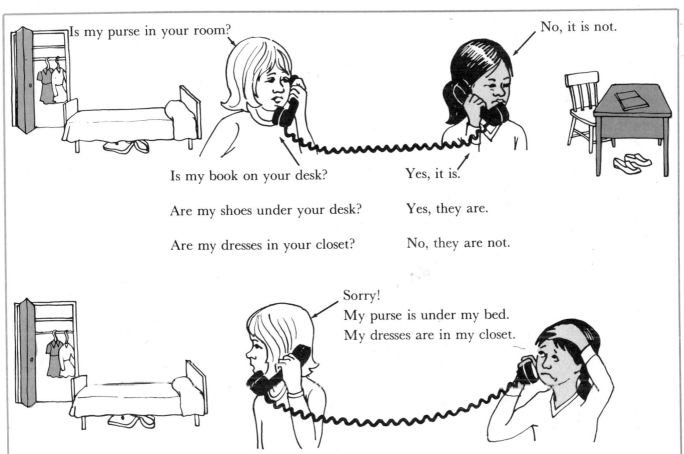

Is my purse in your room?

No, it is not.

Is my book on your desk?

Yes, it is.

Are my shoes under your desk?

Yes, they are.

Are my dresses in your closet?

No, they are not.

Sorry!
My purse is under my bed.
My dresses are in my closet.

self test

Is the dress in the closet?
Yes, it is.

Are the shoes in the box?
No, they are not. They are on the box.

1. Is the purse in the closet?

2. Is the shirt on the belt?

3. Are her shoes on her feet?

4. Are the books on the table?

5. Are the glasses on the floor?

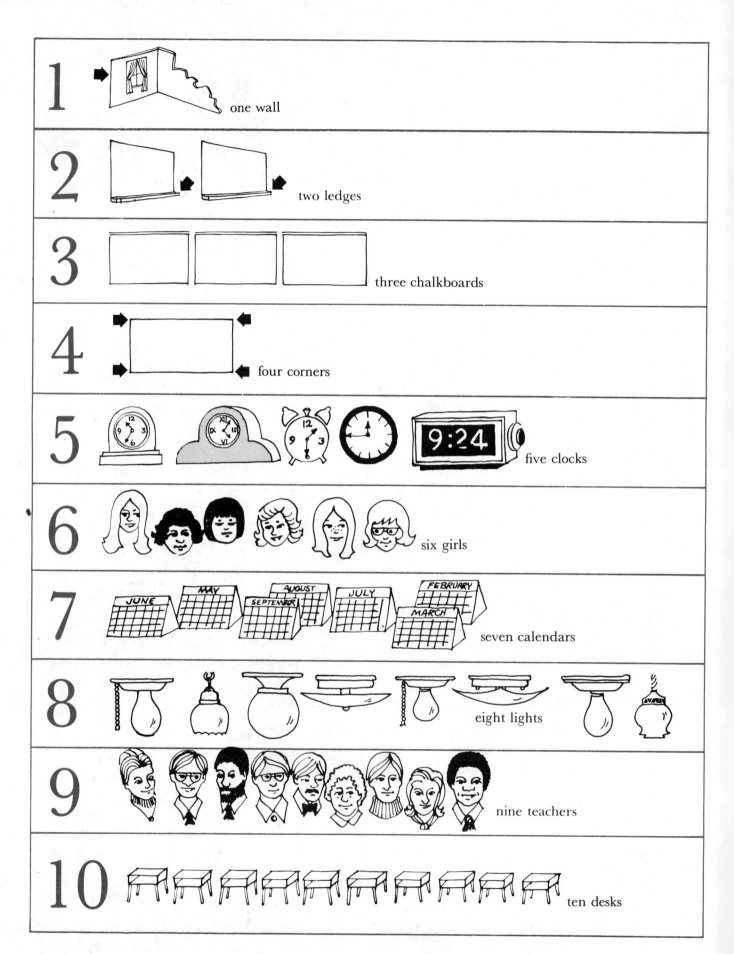

1   one wall

2   two ledges

3   three chalkboards

4   four corners

5   five clocks

6   six girls

7   seven calendars

8   eight lights

9   nine teachers

10   ten desks

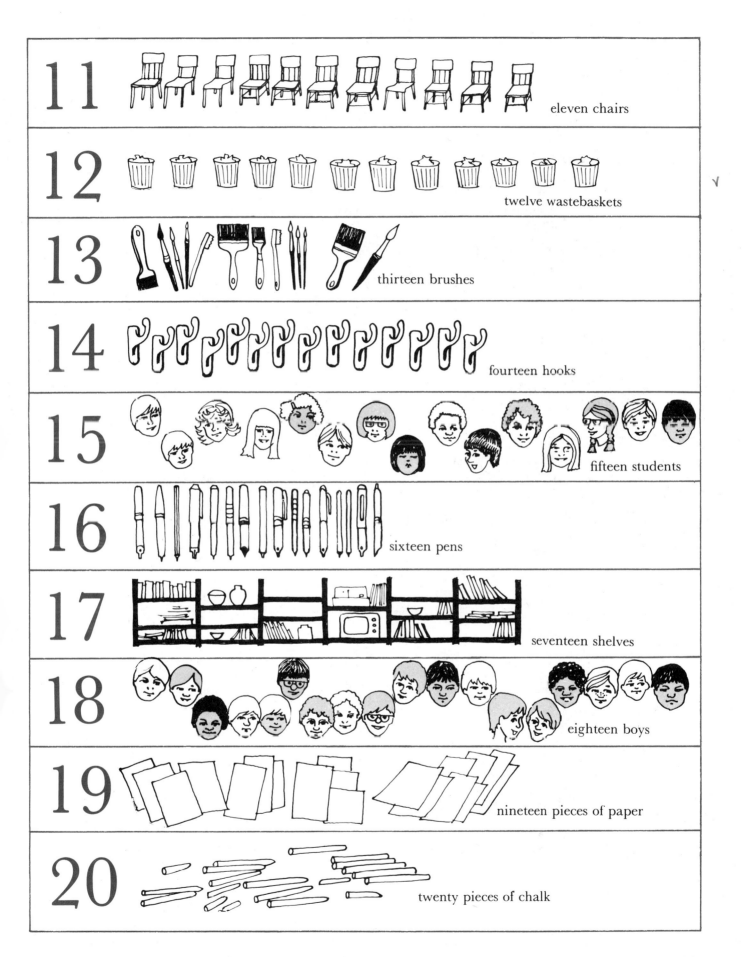

11	eleven chairs
12	twelve wastebaskets
13	thirteen brushes
14	fourteen hooks
15	fifteen students
16	sixteen pens
17	seventeen shelves
18	eighteen boys
19	nineteen pieces of paper
20	twenty pieces of chalk

How many doors are in the room?
There are two doors in the room.

How many windows are in the room?
There are four windows in the room.

How many desks are in the room?
There are six desks in the room.

How many teachers are in the room?
There is one teacher in the room.

How many students are in the room?
There are three students in the room.

How many books are on the shelves?
There are twelve books on the shelves.

How many pencils are on the teacher's desk?
There are eight pencils on the teacher's desk.

How many books are on the teacher's desk?
There are four books on the teacher's desk.

How many chalkboards are in the room?
There is one chalkboard in the room.

How many hooks are in the room?
There are no hooks in the room.*

* OR There are not any hooks in the room. OR There aren't any hooks in the room.

How many?

How many pencils are on the student's desk?

There is one pencil on the student's desk.

How many books are in the student's hands?

There is one book in the student's hands.

How many books are on the student's desk?

There are two books on the student's desk.

How many pencils are on the students' desks?

There are three pencils on the students' desks.

How many books are on the students' desks?

There are four books on the students' desks.

How many books are in the students' hands?

There are two books in the students' hands.

What is in this picture?

Are there any chairs in this picture?
Yes, there are some chairs in this picture.

How many chairs are there?
There are two.

Are there any books in this picture?
Yes, there are some books in this picture.

How many books are there?
There are three.

Are there any students in this picture?
Yes, there are some students in this picture.

How many students are there?
There are four.

Are there any calendars in this picture?
No, there are not any calendars in this picture.

What is in this closet?

Are there any dresses in this closet?
Yes, there are some dresses in this closet.

How many dresses are there?
There are three.

Are there any pairs of pants in this closet?
Yes, there are some pairs of pants in this closet.

How many pairs of pants are there?
There are two.

Are there any pairs of shoes in this closet?
Yes, there are some pairs of shoes in this closet.

How many pairs of shoes are there?
There are three.

Are there any pairs of jeans in this closet?
No, there are not any pairs of jeans in this closet.

Is there a coat in this closet?
Yes, there is a coat in this closet. OR
Yes, there is.

Is there a skirt in this closet?
No, there is not a skirt in this closet. OR
No, there is not.

What is in these pictures?

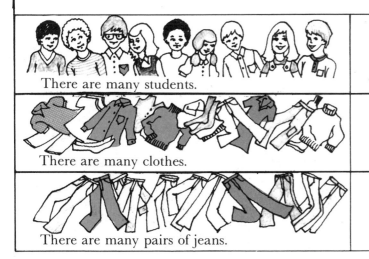

There are many students.

There are a few students.

There are many clothes.

There are a few clothes.

There are many pairs of jeans.

There are a few pairs of jeans.

What is in this picture?

What is in this picture?

1. Are there any students in this room?
2. Are there any books on the shelves?
3. Is there a calendar on the wall?
4. Are there any pencils in the box?
5. Is there a ledge in this room?
6. Are there any chalkboards in this room?
7. Are there any erasers in this room?
8. Is there a door in this room?

9. Are there any windows in this room?
10. Is there a teacher on a chair?
11. How many teachers are in the room?
12. How many calendars are on the wall?
13. How many books are on the shelves?
14. How many students are in the room?
15. How many pencils are in the box?

unit four

B	I	N	G	O
1	21	41	61	81
3	24	44	65	83
12	30	●	70	87
15	36	54	77	94
20	40	60	80	99

B	I	N	G	O
2	22	42	62	82
7	23	45	64	86
10	26	●	72	89
14	34	50	75	93
19	39	59	79	98

10 ten	60 sixty	100 one hundred	20 twenty	100 one hundred
20 twenty	70 seventy	200 two hundred	21 twenty-one	101 one hundred one
30 thirty	80 eighty	300 three hundred	22 twenty-two	102 one hundred two
40 forty	90 ninety	1000 one thousand	23 twenty-three	103 one hundred three
50 fifty		2000 two thousand		
		3000 three thousand		

What time is it?

7:00 a.m.

It is seven o'clock.

7:05 a.m.

It is five minutes after seven.

7:10 a.m.

It is ten minutes after seven.

Good morning.

7:15 a.m.

It is fifteen minutes after seven. OR
It is a quarter after seven.

7:40 a.m.

It is seven forty. OR
It is twenty minutes to eight.

7:20 a.m.

It is twenty minutes after seven.

7:45 a.m.

It is seven forty-five. OR
It is a quarter to eight.

7:25 a.m.

It is twenty-five minutes after seven.

7:50 a.m.

It is seven fifty. OR
It is ten minutes to eight.

7:30 a.m.

It is seven thirty. OR
It is half past seven.

7:55 a.m.

It is seven fifty-five. OR
It is five minutes to eight.

7:35 a.m.

It is seven thirty-five. OR
It is twenty-five minutes to eight.

8:00 a.m.

It is eight o'clock.

Good afternoon.

12:00 p.m.

It is twelve o'clock.
OR
It is noon.

12:30 p.m.

It is twelve thirty.

6:45 p.m.

It is a quarter to seven.

Good evening.

12:00 a.m.

It is twelve o'clock. OR
It is midnight.

Good night.

I am waking up.

I wake up every morning.

I am washing my face.
I wash my face every morning.

I am brushing my teeth.
I brush my teeth every morning.

I am putting on my clothes.
I put on my clothes every morning.

I am combing my hair.
I comb my hair every morning.

I am eating breakfast.
I eat breakfast every morning.

I am clearing the table.
I clear the table every morning.

Do you comb your hair every morning?

Yes, I comb my hair every morning. OR

Yes, I do.

Do you wash your hair every morning?

No, I do not wash my hair every morning. OR

No, I do not.*

*do not OR don't

What does she do every morning?
She wakes up every morning.

What does he do every morning?
He eats breakfast every morning.

What does he do every afternoon?
He eats lunch every afternoon.

What does she do every afternoon?
She reads a book every afternoon.

What do you do every afternoon?
We do our homework every afternoon.

What do they do every afternoon?
They do their homework every afternoon.

What does she do every evening?
She watches TV every evening.

What do they do every evening?
They watch TV every evening.

What does he do every evening?
He eats supper every evening.

What do you do every night?
We go to bed every night.

What do they do every afternoon?

① ②

What does she do every evening?

③  ④

What does he do every night?

⑤ ⑥

When? OR What time?

 When do you eat breakfast? OR
What time do you eat breakfast?  I eat breakfast at 7:15.

 When does Bob eat lunch? OR
What time does Bob eat lunch?  He eats lunch at noon.

 When does Kate do her homework? OR
What time does Kate do her homework? She does her homework at 3:45.

 When do Bob and Kate eat supper? OR
What time do Bob and Kate
eat supper?  Bob and Kate eat supper
at 6 o'clock. OR
They eat supper at 6 o'clock.

36

Meat

This is a steer.

This is beef.

What does beef come from?
Beef comes from steers.

This is a sheep.

This is lamb.

What does lamb come from?
Lamb comes from sheep.

Eggs

This is a chicken.

This is chicken.

This is an egg.

What do eggs come from?
Eggs come from chickens.

Fish

This is a fish.

This is fish.

Milk

This is a cow.

This is milk.

This is a glass of milk.

What does milk come from?
Milk comes from cows.

Vegetables

This is corn.

This is spinach.

This is a carrot.

This is a potato.

This is a tomato.

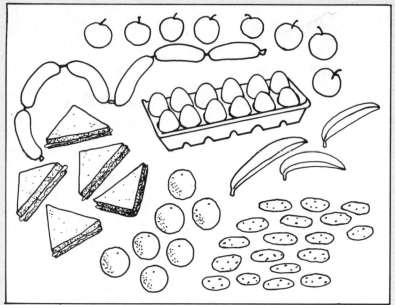

How many _____ do you want?

sausages
eggs
sandwiches
cookies
apples
bananas
oranges

I want one _____ .OR

I would like one _____ :

sausage
egg
sandwich
cookie
apple
banana
orange

How much _____ do you want?

cereal
soup
toast
juice
milk
water
cake
meat
corn
bread
candy
pop

I want one _____ of _____: OR
I would like one _____ of _____:

bowl   cereal
           soup

piece   toast
           cake
           candy

glass   juice
           milk
           water

bottle   pop

helping   meat
           corn

slice   bread

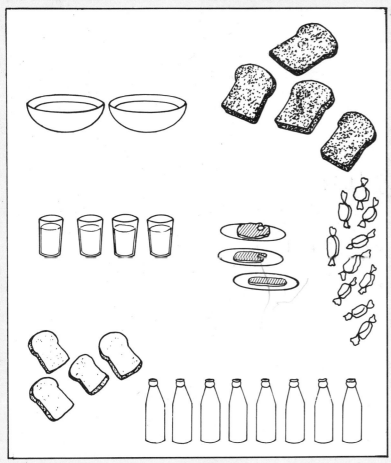

I want _____ _____ of _____: OR
I would like _____ _____ of _____:

bowls   soup
pieces   toast
glasses   water
bottles   pop
helpings   meat
slices   bread
pieces   candy

Do you want any_____?

sausages
eggs
sandwiches
cookies
apples
bananas
oranges

Yes, I want some. OR
Yes, I would like some.

Yes, I want a few. OR
Yes, I would like a few.

Yes, I want a lot. OR
Yes, I would like a lot.

No, I do not want any.

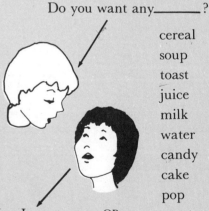

Do you want any_____?

cereal
soup
toast
juice
milk
water
candy
cake
pop
meat
corn
bread

Yes, I want some. OR
Yes, I would like some.

Yes, I want a little. OR
Yes, I would like a little.

Yes, I want a lot. OR
Yes, I would like a lot.

No, I do not want any.

never   sometimes   usually   always

What do you have for breakfast?

I sometimes have a bowl of cereal.

I always have a glass of juice.

I never have any cookies.

I never have any cake.

What do you have for lunch?

I usually have a bowl of soup.

I usually have a sandwich.

I always have a glass of milk.

What do you have for a snack?

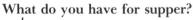

I sometimes have a bottle of pop.

I sometimes have an orange.

What do you have for supper?

I usually have a helping of meat.

I sometimes have a slice of bread.

I usually have two helpings of corn.

I always have a glass of water.

unit five

PRONUNCIATION

◀ She is feeling the box.

She is filling the box. ▶

◀ He is picking up the crib.

He is picking up the crab. ▶

◀ Mix a pancake,
Stir a pancake,
   Pop it in the pan;
Fry the pancake, ▶
Toss the pancake,
   Catch it if you can.

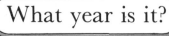

What year is it?

It is 1878.

It is 1978.   19   78
nineteen seventy-eight

What month is it?

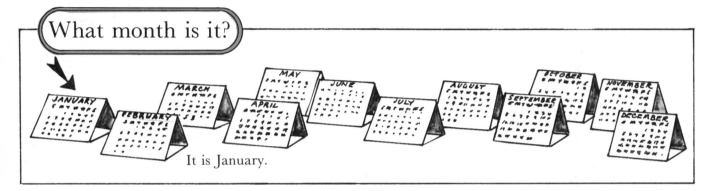

It is January.

week

| Monday | Tuesday | Wednesday | Thursday | Friday | Saturday | Sunday |

weekdays — weekend

What day is today?

It is Tuesday.

What day is tomorrow?
It is Wednesday.

What day was yesterday?
It was Monday.

Today's date is January 15th. OR
It is January 15th. OR
It is the 15th.

Tomorrow's date is January 16th. OR
It is January 16th. OR
It is the 16th.

Kate: When is your birthday?
Bob: It is June 9th.

JANUARY

S	M	T	W	Th	F	S
					1	2	3	4	5
6	7	8	9	10	11	12
13	14	(15)	16	17	18	19
20	21	22	23	24	25	26
27	28	29	30	31

1st	**first**	1	one	6th	six**th**	6	six	13th	thirteen**th**	13	thirteen
2nd	**second**	2	two	7th	seven**th**	7	seven	20th	twent**ieth**	20	twenty
3rd	**third**	3	three	8th	eigh**th**	8	eight	21st	twenty-**first**	21	twenty-one
4th	four**th**	4	four	9th	nin**th**	9	nine	30th	thir**tieth**	30	thirty
5th	fif**th**	5	five	10th	ten**th**	10	ten	31st	thirty-**first**	31	thirty-one

She is going to school now.
She goes to school every weekday.

He is going home now.
He goes home every day.

She is going to the grocery store now.
She goes to the grocery store every Tuesday.

He is going to the supermarket now.
He goes to the supermarket every Saturday.

She is going to the drugstore now.
She goes to the drugstore every Friday.

They are going to the library now.
They go to the library every week.

They are going to a restaurant now.
They go to a restaurant every weekend.

They are going to a gas station now.
They go to a gas station every week.

They are going to a movie now.
They go to a movie every Sunday.

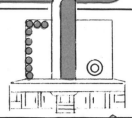

They are going to a concert now.
They go to a concert every weekend.

They are going to a basketball game now.
They go to a basketball game every Friday.

They are going to a soccer game now.
They go to a soccer game every Saturday.

They are going to a hockey game now.
They go to a hockey game every weekend.

They are going to a baseball game now.
They go to a baseball game every Thursday.

She is going to a swimming meet now.
She goes to a swimming meet every Saturday.

They are going to a party now.
They go to a party every weekend.

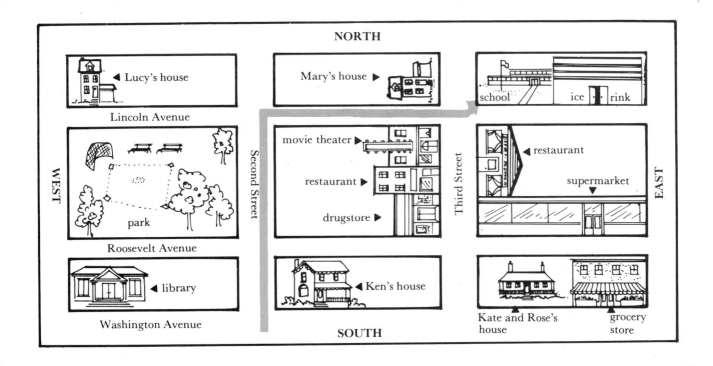

NORTH

Lucy's house ◄

Lincoln Avenue

Mary's house ►

school | ice · rink

WEST

park

Second Street

movie theater ►

restaurant ►

drugstore ►

Third Street

restaurant ◄

supermarket ▼

EAST

Roosevelt Avenue

library ◄

Washington Avenue

Ken's house ◄

Kate and Rose's house

grocery store

SOUTH

How do you get to school?

Lucy

I always walk
First I go up Second Street for two blocks.
Then I turn right.
I go east along Lincoln Avenue for a block.
Then I cross Lincoln Avenue.
Then I am at school

Ken

How does Lucy get to school?

She usually walks.
She goes east along Lincoln Avenue for two blocks.
Then she is at school.

How do you get to the movie theater?

Mary

Kate

Rose

We usually walk.
First we go west along Washington Avenue.
Then we turn right.
We go north up Third Street for two blocks.
Then we cross Third Street.
Then we are at the movie theater.

47

How does she get to school? — How does he get to school?

She always walks.

She usually goes by bus. OR
By bus.

He sometimes goes by car. OR
By car.

He sometimes goes by taxi. OR
By taxi.

She sometimes goes by truck. OR
By truck.

He always goes by train. OR
By train.

He always rides his bicycle.

She usually rides her horse.

Coming and going

The girl is going out.
The boy is coming in.

She is going to school.

He is coming to school.

Does he go to school by bus?

No, he does not.*

He goes by plane.

Does she walk to school?

No, she does not. She rides her horse to school.

Does she walk to school?

Yes, she walks to school. OR Yes, she does.

Do they go to school by train?

No, they do not. They go to school by bus.

Do they go to school by boat?

Yes, they go to school by boat. OR Yes, they do.

*does not OR doesn't

unit six

PRONUNCIATION

◄ He is holding a pin.
He is holding a pen. ►

◄ She is sitting on a pole.
She is sitting on a bowl. ►

Peter Piper picked a peck of pickled peppers;
A peck of pickled peppers Peter Piper picked.
If Peter Piper picked a peck of pickled peppers,
Where's the peck of pickled peppers Peter Piper picked?

My family

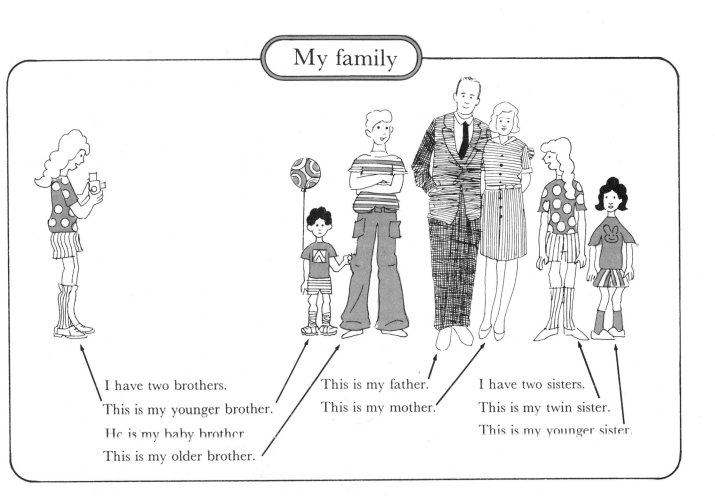

I have two brothers.

This is my younger brother.

He is my baby brother.

This is my older brother.

This is my father.

This is my mother.

I have two sisters.

This is my twin sister.

This is my younger sister.

My relatives

I have many cousins.

Those are my cousins.

Those are my aunts.

Those are my uncles.

Those are my grandmothers.

Those are my grandfathers.

Do you have any brothers?

No, I do not have any brothers. OR
No, I do not.

Do you have any sisters?

No, I do not have any sisters. OR
No, I do not.

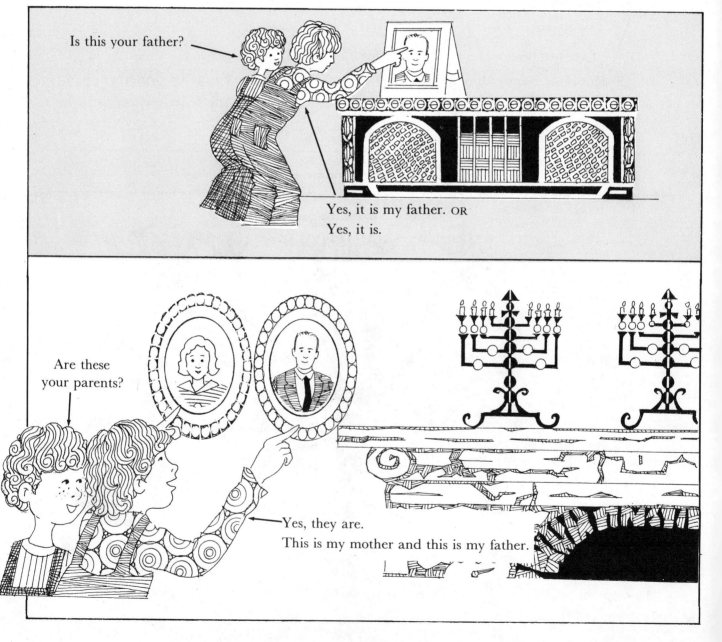

Is this your father?

Yes, it is my father. OR
Yes, it is.

Are these your parents?

Yes, they are.
This is my mother and this is my father.

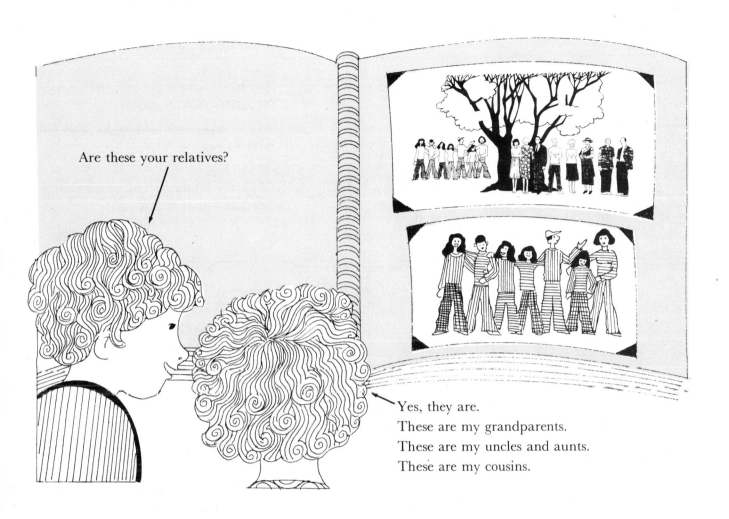

Are these your relatives?

Yes, they are.
These are my grandparents.
These are my uncles and aunts.
These are my cousins.

Is this your father?

It is my stepfather.

Are these your parents?

These are my foster parents.
This is Shirley and this is Victor.

How old are you?

I am twelve years old. OR
I am twelve.
My older sister is sixteen years old. OR
My older sister is sixteen.
My younger sisters are eight years old and six years old. OR
My younger sisters are eight and six.
My baby brother is two years old. OR
My baby brother is two.

I am older than you are. OR
I am older than you.

I am younger than you are. OR
I am younger than you.

My grandfather is eighty years old.
He is the oldest person in our family.

My baby brother is two years old.
He is the youngest person in our family.

1. How old are you?

2. How many brothers do you have?
   How old are they?

3. How many sisters do you have?
   How old are they?

4. Do you have any older brothers?
   Do you have any younger brothers?

5. Do you have any older sisters?
   Do you have any younger sisters?

6. Who is the oldest person in your family?
   Who is the youngest person in your family?

How tall are you?

100 cm	one hundred centimeters
101 cm	one hundred one centimeters
150 cm	one hundred fifty centimeters
151 cm	one hundred fifty-one centimeters
151.5 cm	one hundred fifty-one point five centimeters
150.9 cm	one hundred fifty point nine centimeters

I am 151 cm tall.

I am 153 cm tall.
I am taller than you are. OR
I am taller than you. OR
I am taller.

Which girl is taller?

Which girl is taller?

The second girl is taller than the first girl. OR
The second girl is taller. OR
The second one is taller.

Which one is the tallest?

Which tree is the tallest?

The second tree is the tallest. OR
The second one is the tallest.

Which boy is the tallest?

The third boy is the tallest. OR
The third one is the tallest.

Which girl is the tallest?

The fifth girl is the tallest. OR
The fifth one is the tallest.

How high is it?

This fence is 104 cm high.

This fence is 99 cm high.

The first fence is higher than the second fence.

Which one is higher?

Which shelf is higher?

The top shelf is higher
than the bottom shelf. OR

The top shelf is higher. OR

The top one is higher.

Which boy is higher?

The first boy is higher
than the second boy. OR

The first boy is higher. OR

The first one is higher.

How long is it?

This pencil is 14 cm long.

The first pencil is longer than the second pencil.

This pencil is 10 cm long.

Which one is longer?

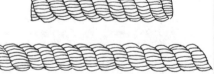

Which line is longer?

The first line is longer OR
than the second line.

The first line is longer. OR

The first one is longer.

Which girl's hair is longer?

The first girl's hair is longer
than the second girl's hair. OR

The first girl's hair is longer. OR

The first one's hair is longer.

Which rope is longer?

The second rope is longer
than the first rope. OR

The second rope is longer. OR

The second one is longer.

How thick is it?

This book is 5 cm thick.

This book is 2 cm thick.

The first book is thicker than the second book.

Which one is thicker?

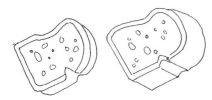

Which slice of bread is thicker?

The second slice of bread is thicker than the first slice of bread. OR

The second slice of bread is thicker. OR
The second one is thicker.

Which bush is thicker?

The second bush is thicker than the first bush. OR

The second bush is thicker. OR
The second one is thicker.

How wide is it?

This door is 84 cm wide.

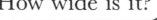

This door is 50 cm wide.

The first door is wider than the second door.

Which one is wider?

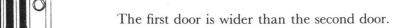

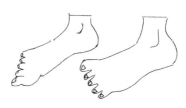

Which bed is wider?

The first bed is wider than the second bed. OR
The first bed is wider. OR
The first one is wider.

Which foot is wider?

The second foot is wider than the first foot. OR
The second foot is wider. OR
The second one is wider.

How big is it?

This piece of paper is 4 cm by 2.5 cm.   This piece of paper is 2.5 cm by 1 cm.

The first piece of paper is bigger than the second piece of paper.

Which one is bigger?

Which ball is bigger?

The soccer ball is bigger
than the baseball. OR
The soccer ball is bigger.

Which hand is bigger?

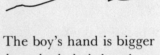

The boy's hand is bigger
than the baby's hand. OR
The boy's hand is bigger.

self test

long

Which rope is longer?

The first rope is longer than the second rope.

wide

Which car is the widest?
The fourth car is the widest.

high
①
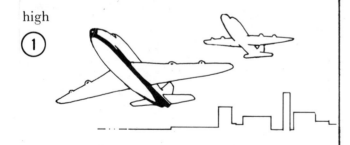

big
②
  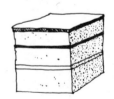

tall
③

thick
④
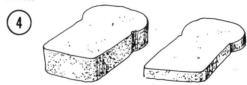

long
⑤

Which boy is taller?
Neither. They are the same height.

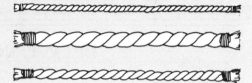

Which rope is the longest?
None. They are the same length.

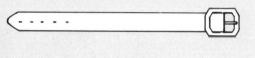

Which belt is wider?
Neither. They are the same width.

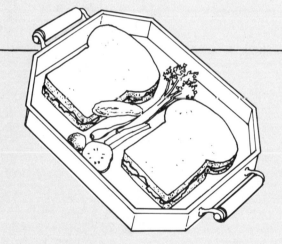

Which sandwich is thicker?
Neither. They are the same thickness.

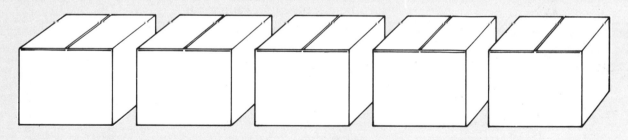

Which box is the biggest?
None. They are the same size.

unit seven

PRONUNCIATION

◀ Sheep should not sleep in a shoe.

Sheep should sleep in a shed. ▶

How many cans can a canner can
If a canner can can cans?
A canner can can as many cans
As a canner can
If a canner can can cans.

VOCABULARY

What do you see in this picture?

I see **the moon**.

Where is **the moon**?

It is in the sky. OR
The moon is in the sky.

I see **a star**.

Where is **the star**?

It is in the sky. OR
The star is in the sky.

What do you see in this picture?

I see the sun.

I see a girl.

I see some clouds. OR
I see three clouds.

I see some fish. OR
I see three fish.

I see a house.

I see some flowers. OR
I see eleven flowers.

I see a lake.

I see a truck.

I see some planes. OR
I see two planes.

I see a tree.

I see a sheep.

I see some cars. OR
I see four cars.

I see some birds. OR
I see six birds.

I see a nest.

I see a road.

I see a dog.

Where is the girl?
She is in a cloud.

Where should she be?
She should be on the ground.

Where is the sun?
It is in the sky.

Should it be in the sky?
Yes, it should be in the sky. OR
Yes, it should.

Should the cars be on the road?
Yes, they should be on the road. OR
Yes, they should.

Should the sheep be in the tree?
No, it should not* be in the tree. OR
No, it should not.

Should the fish be in the sky?
No, they should not be in the sky. OR
No, they should not.

Where is the nest?
It is on the car.

Where should it be?
It should be in the tree.

Where are the flowers?
They are on the roof.

Where should they be?
They should be in the ground.

Where are the planes?
They are in the lake. OR
They are in the water.

Where should they be?
They should be in the sky.

* should not OR shouldn't

His shirt is on backwards. OR
His shirt is backwards.

Her head is on upside down. OR
Her head is upside down.

(1)

(2)

(3)

(4)

(5)

Should he open the door?
No, he should not.

Should she wash her face?
Yes, she should.

Should she put on her shoes now?
No, she should not.

Should he clear the table?
Yes, he should.

Should you put on your coat?
Yes, I should.

Should you drink this water?
No, I should not.

Should you sit on this chair?

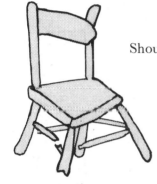

① 1

Should she close her mouth?

③ 3

Should he take off his shoes?

② 2

Should he open a window?

④ 4

⑤ 5

Should she go to a grocery store?

Can you pick up your teacher's desk?

No, I cannot* pick up my teacher's desk. OR
No, I cannot.

Can you touch the chalkboard?

Yes, I can touch the chalkboard. OR
Yes, I can.

Can you carry twenty books?

No, I cannot carry twenty books. OR
No, I cannot.

Can you carry five books?

Yes, I can carry five books. OR
Yes, I can.

A snake can crawl.

A bird can fly.

A snake cannot fly.

This boy can play the piano.

This girl can sing songs.

This girl cannot play the guitar.

A fish can swim.

A person can walk.

* cannot OR can't

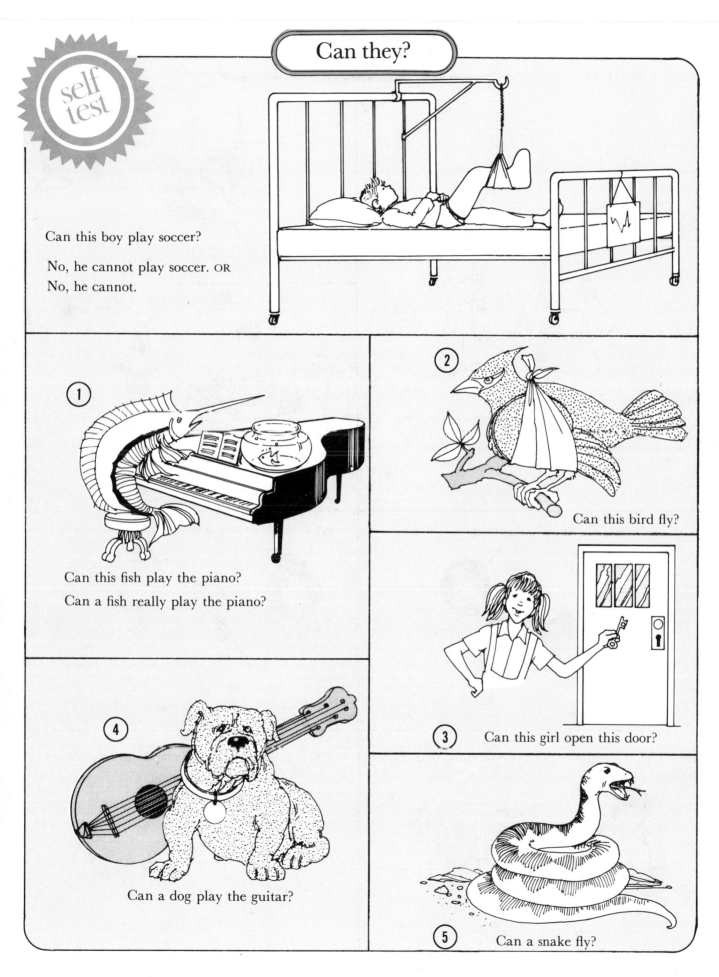

Can this boy play soccer?

No, he cannot play soccer. OR
No, he cannot.

① Can this fish play the piano?
Can a fish really play the piano?

② Can this bird fly?

③ Can this girl open this door?

④ Can a dog play the guitar?

⑤ Can a snake fly?

What is it made of?

What is your dress made of?

It is made of cloth.

What are your shoes made of?

They are made of leather.

What is your desk made of?

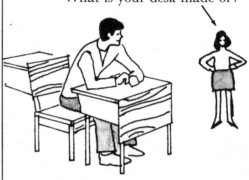

It is made of wood.

What is your purse made of?

It is made of vinyl.

What is your pen made of?

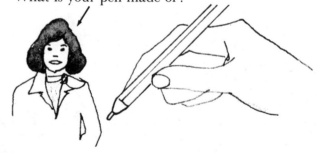

It is made of plastic.

What is your wristwatch made of?

It is made of metal.

What is your sweater made of?

It is made of acrylic.

Game time

I can move four squares.
You can move two squares.

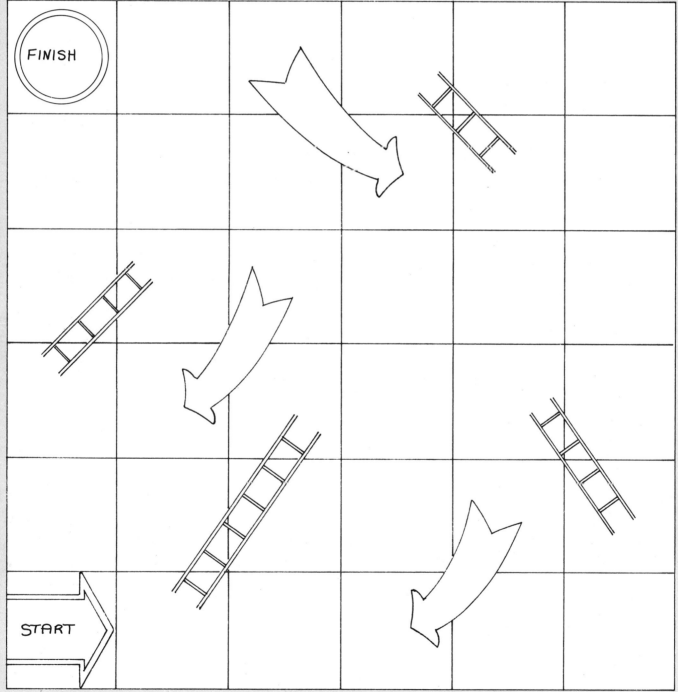

unit eight

PRONUNCIATION

She has two decks. ▲

She has two ducks. ▼

The man cannot walk. ▲

The men cannot walk. ▼

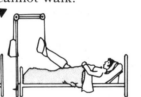

Do not pinch me. ▲

Do not punch me. ▼

Betty Botter bought some butter,
But, she said, the butter's bitter;
If I put it in my batter
It will make my batter bitter.
But a bit of better butter,
That would make my batter better.

So she bought a bit of butter
Better than her bitter butter,
And she put it in her batter
And the batter was not bitter.
So it was better Betty Botter
Bought a bit of better butter.

When do you usually wake up?

I usually wake up at 7:00.

When do you eat breakfast?

I usually eat breakfast at 7:30.
I wake up before I eat breakfast. OR
I eat breakfast after I wake up.

Paul puts on his socks.
Then Paul puts on his shoes.

He puts on his socks before he puts on his shoes. OR
He puts on his shoes after he puts on his socks.

These students take off their coats. Then they sit down.

These students take off their coats
before they sit down. OR
These students sit down after they
take off their coats.

abcdefg
hijklmn
opqrstu
vwxyz

Does C come before B?

No, C does not come before B. OR
No, it does not.
C comes after B.

Does E come after F?

No, E does not come after F. OR
No, it does not.
E comes before F.

1 2 3 4 5
6 7 8 9 10

Does 2 come before 8?

Yes, 2 comes before 8. OR
Yes, it does.

Does 7 come after 6?

Yes, 7 comes after 6. OR
Yes, it does.

Carol's class schedule

	Monday, Wednesday, Friday	Tuesday, Thursday
9:00 a.m.	Spanish language	Spanish language
10:00 a.m.	recess	recess
10:15 a.m.	mathematics	mathematics
11:00 a.m.	English language	English language
12:00 p.m.	lunch	lunch
1:00 p.m.	social studies	science
1:45 p.m.	music	art
2:15 p.m.	recess	recess
2:30 p.m.	physical education	health education
3:15 p.m.	home economics	industrial arts

Carol has music before she has recess every Monday, Wednesday, and Friday.
Carol has health education after she has recess every Tuesday and Thursday.

Do you see…?

I see it.

I see it.

I see it.

I see it.

I see it.

I see them.

I see her.   I see her.   I see him.   I see him.

He sees me.

I see you.

I see you.

I see myself.

I see myself.

A Detective Story

It is eating me up.

It ate me up.

First I came in the room.
Then I grabbed the girl and ate her up.

What happened?

My child disappeared.

Look at this. I see a footprint.
It is not a human being's footprint.
It is a monster's footprint.

Let's find that monster.
Let's save your child.

How can we save your child?

We can tickle the monster.

I saw a footprint.
It was not a human being's footprint.
It was a monster's footprint.
We found the monster.
We tickled it.
We saved you.

What happened?

The girl closed the door.
Then she opened the window.
A monster came in the room.
It grabbed the girl.
It ate her up.

What is he doing?	What did he do?
He is carrying twenty books.	He carried twenty books.
He is clearing his desk.	He cleared his desk.
He is touching the ceiling.	He touched the ceiling.
He is walking to school.	He walked to school.
He is washing his socks.	He washed his socks.
He is picking up his desk.	He picked up his desk.

What is she doing? | What did she do?

She is sitting down.

She sat down.

She is putting on her shoes.

She put on her shoes.

She is taking off her sweater.

She took off her sweater.

She is going to school by plane.

She went to school by plane.

What did they do?

What did he do?

He opened the door.   Then he closed it.

What did she do?

She washed her hair.   Then she combed it.

What did they do?

They got their books.   Then they opened them.

What did he do?

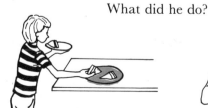 

He got some sandwiches.   Then he ate them.

He	picked up	a book.		Did	he	pick up	a book?
He	picked	a book up.		Did	he	pick	a book up?
He	picked	it	up.	Did	he	pick	it	up?

Did he pick up a book? OR   Yes, he picked it up.
Did he pick a book up?

Did he put on his shirt? OR   Yes, he put it on.
Did he put his shirt on?

Did he take off his belt? OR   Yes, he took it off.
Did he take his belt off?

Yes, she picked them up.

Did she pick up two pencils? OR
Did she pick two pencils up?

Did she put on her shoes? OR
Did she put her shoes on?

Yes, she put them on.

Did he take off his jeans? OR   No, he did not*take them off.
Did he take his jeans off?   He took off his socks. OR
He took his socks off.

*did not OR didn't

78

Did he put on his shoes? OR
Did he put his shoes on?

No, he did not put them on.
He put on his pants. OR
He put his pants on.

Did she pick up three pencils? OR
Did she pick three pencils up?

No, she did not pick them up.
She put them down.

Did our teacher hand out an assignment? OR
Did our teacher hand an assignment out?

No, she did not hand one out.
She handed out some books. OR
She handed some books out.

Did you hand in your assignment? OR
Did you hand your assignment in?

No, I did not hand in my assignment. OR
No, I did not hand it in.

Please turn on the lights. OR
Please turn the lights on. OR
Please turn them on.

Please turn off the lights. OR
Please turn the lights off. OR
Please turn them off.

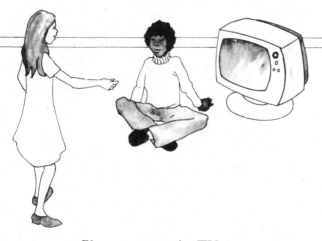

Please turn on the TV. OR
Please turn the TV on. OR
Please turn it on.

Please turn off the TV. OR
Please turn the TV off. OR
Please turn it off.

radio

stereo

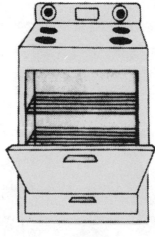

oven

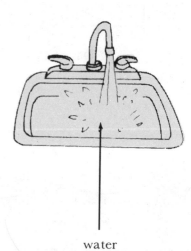

water

unit nine

A tutor who tooted the flute

A **Tut**or who **toot**ed the **flute**
Tried to **teach** two young **toot**ers to **toot**;
Said the **two** to the **Tut**or,
"Is it **hard**er to **toot**, or
To **tut**or two **toot**ers to **toot**?"

81

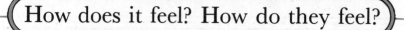

How does it feel? How do they feel?

Touch my sweater.
How does it feel?

It feels soft.

Touch the floor.
How does it feel?

It feels smooth.
It feels hard.

Touch the ground.
How does it feel?

It feels rough.

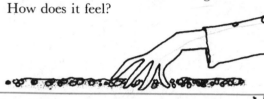

Touch my knuckles.
How do they feel?

They feel bumpy.

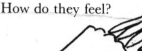

Touch this stone.
How does it feel?

It feels hot.

Touch this stone.
How does it feel?

It feels cold.

Touch your tongue.
How does it feel?

It feels wet.

Touch a book.
How does it feel?

It feels dry.

How did it feel? How did they feel?

How did her hair feel?

It felt soft.

How did her hands feel?

They felt rough.

82

How does it look? How do they look?

Look at the sky.
How does it look?

It looks dark.

Look at the sky.
How does it look?

It looks light.

Look at this can.
How does it look?
It looks shiny.

Look at this glass.
How does it look?

It looks dull.

Look at these hands.
How do they look?

They look dirty.

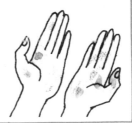

Look at these hands.
How do they look?

They look clean.

How does it smell?

Smell this meat.
How does it smell?

It smells good.

Smell this fish.
How does it smell?

It smells bad.

How did it look?

How did the toast look?

It looked dark.

How did it smell?

How did that meat smell?

It smelled bad.

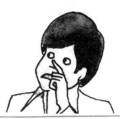

1 Does this boy's hair look light or dark?
Do his shoes look shiny or dull?

2 Do these clothes look wet or dry?
Do they look clean or dirty?

3 Does the road look bumpy or smooth?
Do the tires on the car look hard or soft?

tire

4 Does this person look hot or cold?

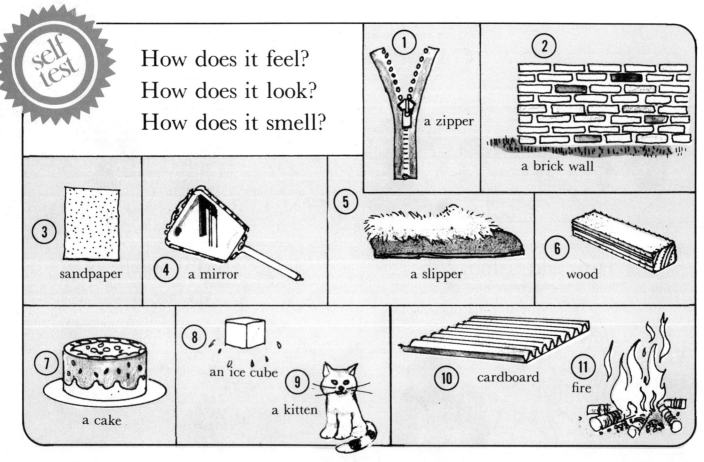

How does it feel?
How does it look?
How does it smell?

1 a zipper

2 a brick wall

3 sandpaper

4 a mirror

5 a slipper

6 wood

7 a cake

8 an ice cube

9 a kitten

10 cardboard

11 fire

84

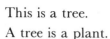

These are plants.

This is a tree.
A tree is a plant.
It has branches.
It has leaves.
It has a trunk.
Bark is on the trunk.
It has roots.

This is a leaf.

These are leaves.

This is a flower.
A flower is a plant.
It has petals.
It has leaves.
It has a stem.
It has roots.

This is grass.
Grass is a plant.
This is a blade of grass.
It has roots.

These are minerals.

These are rocks or stones.

This is soil.

Plants grow in the soil.
Stones and rocks are in the soil.

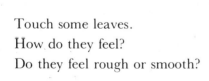

How do they look?
Do they look dark or light?
Do they look shiny or dull?

These leaves do not look light.
They look dark.
They do not look dull.
They look shiny.

How do they smell?
Do they smell good or bad?
These leaves have no smell.

Touch some leaves.
How do they feel?
Do they feel rough or smooth?

These leaves do not feel rough.
They feel smooth.

 This jacket is made of cloth.

 What kind of jacket is that?
It is a cloth jacket.

 This jacket is made of leather.

 What kind of jacket is that?
It is a leather jacket.

 These shoes are made of canvas.

 What kind of shoes are those?
They are canvas shoes.

 This bookcase is made of wood.

 What kind of bookcase is that?
It is a wooden bookcase.

 These walls are made of concrete block.

 What kind of walls are those?
They are concrete block walls.

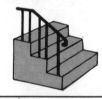 These stairs are made of concrete.

 What kind of stairs are those?
They are concrete stairs.

 This floor is made of tile.

 What kind of floor is that?
It is a tile floor.

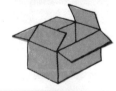 This box is made of cardboard.

 What kind of box is that?
It is a cardboard box.

 This jar is made of glass.

 What kind of jar is that?
It is a glass jar.

What kind of bottle is this?
It is a glass bottle.

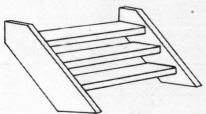

1. What kind of stairs are these?

2. What kind of shoes are these?

3. What kind of telephone is this?

4. What kind of house is this?

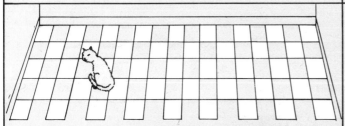

5. What kind of floor is this?

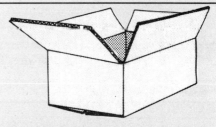

6. What kind of box is this?

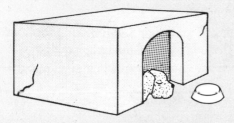

7. What kind of doghouse is this?

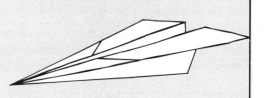

8. What kind of airplane is this?

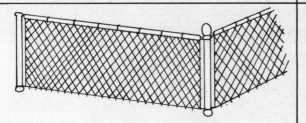

9. What kind of fence is this?

10. What kind of monsters are these?

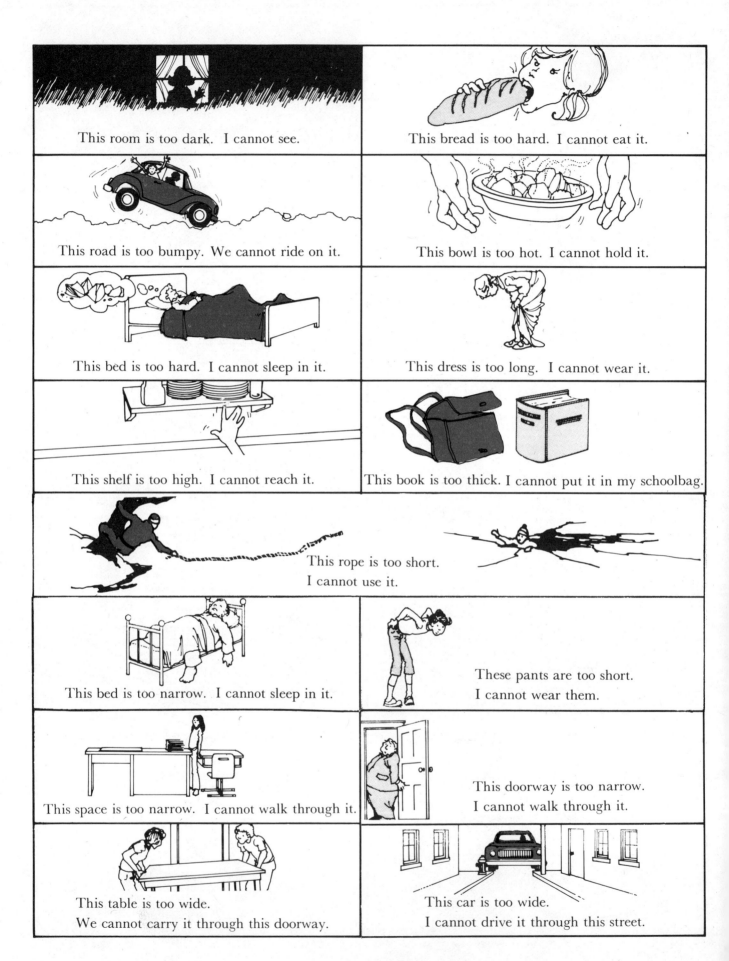

This room is too dark. I cannot see.

This bread is too hard. I cannot eat it.

This road is too bumpy. We cannot ride on it.

This bowl is too hot. I cannot hold it.

This bed is too hard. I cannot sleep in it.

This dress is too long. I cannot wear it.

This shelf is too high. I cannot reach it.

This book is too thick. I cannot put it in my schoolbag.

This rope is too short. I cannot use it.

This bed is too narrow. I cannot sleep in it.

These pants are too short. I cannot wear them.

This space is too narrow. I cannot walk through it.

This doorway is too narrow. I cannot walk through it.

This table is too wide. We cannot carry it through this doorway.

This car is too wide. I cannot drive it through this street.

These jeans are too short.
I cannot wear them.

unit ten

PRONUNCIATION

Song of the train

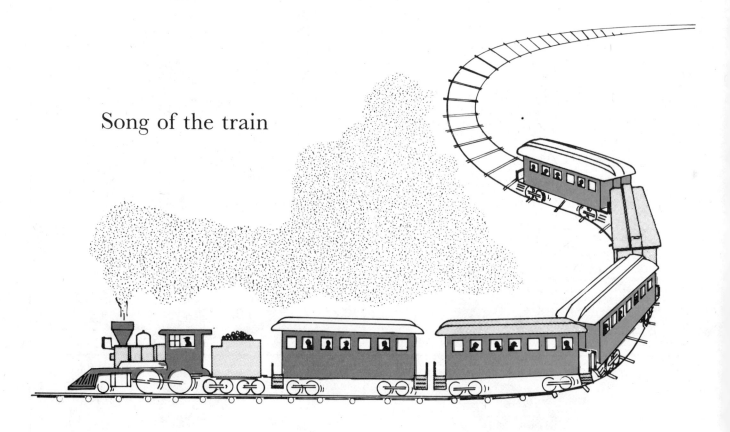

Clickety-clack,
Wheels on the track,
This is the way
They begin the attack:
Click-ety-clack,
Click-ety-clack,
Click-ety, **clack**-ety,
Click-ety
Clack.

Clickety-clack,
Over the crack,
Faster and faster
The song of the track:
Clickety-clack,
Clickety-clack,
Clickety-clackety,
Clackety
Clack.

Riding in front,
Riding in back,
Everyone hears
The song of the track:
Clickety-clack,
Clickety-clack,
Clickety, **clickety,**
Clackety
Clack.

This is a new shirt.

This is an old shirt.

These are new shoes.

These are old shoes.

This is a big hamburger.

This is a little hamburger.

These are big dogs.

These are little dogs.

This is a fat man.

This is a thin man.

These are fat babies.

These are thin babies.

This is a thick rope.

This is a thin rope.

These are thick books.

These are thin books.

This is a heavy box.

This is a light box.

These are heavy coats.

These are light coats.

This is a wet towel.

This is a dry towel.

These are wet cats.

These are dry cats.

This is a sharp knife.

This is a dull knife.

These are sharp knives.

These are dull knives.

These are sharp scissors.

These are dull scissors.

This is a straight line.

This is a crooked line.

This rope is too thin.
We have to get a thicker one.

This chair is too heavy.
I have to get a lighter one.

This cat is too thin.
We have to find a fatter cat.

This jacket is too small.
I have to get a bigger one.

These knives are too dull.
I have to get some sharper ones.

This sign is old.
We have to make a new one.

That table is wet.
We have to find a dry one.

That letter I is crooked.
You have to make
a straight one.

He got a lighter chair.

They got a thicker rope.

She got a bigger jacket.

They found a fatter cat.

She got some sharper knives.

CIRCUS

They made a new sign.

He made a straight letter I.

They found a dry table.

What is the matter? What does he have to do?

What did he do?

find

That dog is too fat.
The boy has to find a thinner one.

He found a thinner one.

1 make

2 find

3 get

What does she have to do? What did she do?

She has to find her shoes.

She found her shoes.

1

2

3

4

5

What do you want to do?

I want to read.

I want to sleep.

I do not want to stand up.

I do not want to sit down

I want to run.

I do not want to jump.

I want to go to the bathroom.

I want to turn the lights off.   I want to turn the lights on.

I want to look in this drawer.

I want to write on the chalkboard.

I want to talk to my teacher.

I want to look out the window.

I want to listen to the radio.   I want to sing.

What does she want to do?

She wants to kick the ball. She wants to catch the ball. She wants to hit the ball.

What does he want to do?

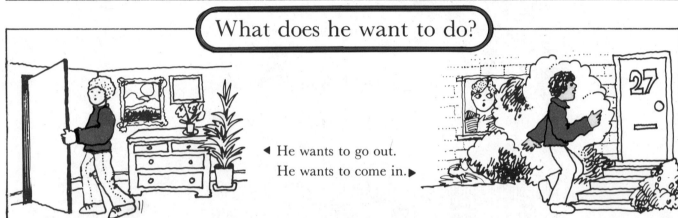

◄ He wants to go out.
He wants to come in. ►

What do you want to do?

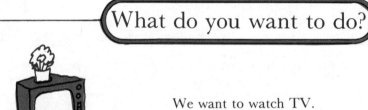

We want to watch TV.

What do they want to do?

They want to turn your radio off.   They want to turn the water on.

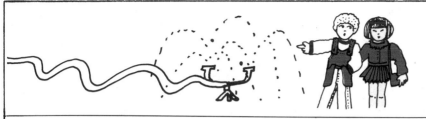

Do you want to turn on the water?

No, I do not want to turn it on. OR
No, I do not.
I want to turn it off.

Does he want to go out?

No, he does not want to go out. OR
No, he does not.

Does he want to stay in the house?

Yes, he wants to stay in the house.
OR
Yes, he does.

What is the length of this line?

This line is 2.3 cm long. OR
This line is two point three centimeters long.

This line is 23 mm long. OR
This line is twenty-three millimeters long.

What is the width of this window?

This window is 1.1 m wide. OR
This window is one point one meters wide.

What is the height of this table?

This table is 1 m high. OR
This table is one meter high.

self test

Measuring things

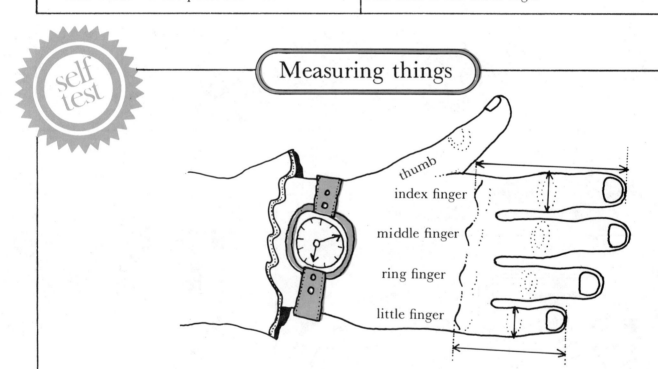

thumb
index finger
middle finger
ring finger
little finger

1. What is the length of this index finger?
2. What is the width of this index finger?
3. What is the length of this little finger?
4. What is the width of this little finger?
5. What is the length of your thumb?

6. What is the length of your ring finger?
7. What is the width of your ring finger?
8. What is the length of your desk?
9. What is the height of your desk?
10. What is the width of your desk?

Are they the same or different?

Victor and Scott are the same height.

Are Victor and Scott the same height?
Yes, they are.

Judy and Gloria weigh the same.

Do Judy and Gloria weigh the same?
Yes, they do.

Are Gloria and Victor the same height?

No, they are not.
They are different heights.
Gloria is taller than Victor.

Do Scott and Judy weigh the same?

No, they do not.
They weigh different amounts.
Scott is heavier than Judy.

unit eleven

Sit down Sister, sit down Brother

Oh, won't you sit down, Sister? I can't sit down. Oh, won't you
Brother

sit down, Sister? I can't sit down. Oh, won't you sit down, Sister? I
Brother Brother

can't sit down, 'Cause I just got to Heaven, Have to look a — round.

Fine

Sit down Sister, sit down Brother

Girls	Boys
Oh, won't you sit down, Brother?	I can't sit down.
Oh, won't you sit down, Brother?	I can't sit down.
Oh, won't you sit down, Brother?	I can't sit down,
	'Cause I just got to Heaven,
	Have to look around.
Oh, won't you sit down, Brother?	I can't sit down.
Oh, won't you sit down, Brother?	I can't sit down.
Oh, won't you sit down, Brother?	I can't sit down.
	'Cause I just got to Heaven,
	Have to look around.

Boys	Girls
Oh, won't you sit down, Sister?	I can't sit down.
Oh, won't you sit down, Sister?	I can't sit down.
Oh, won't you sit down, Sister?	I can't sit down,
	'Cause I just got to Heaven,
	Have to look around.
Oh, won't you sit down, Sister?	I can't sit down.
Oh, won't you sit down, Sister?	I can't sit down.
Oh, won't you sit down, Sister?	I can't sit down.
	'Cause I just got to Heaven,
	Have to look around.

Linda, please pick up the eraser and put it on the ledge.

 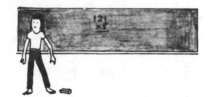 

Stop.
Class, what did Linda do?

She picked up the eraser.

Class, what will Linda do?

She will put the eraser on the ledge.

Mark, please write your name on the chalkboard.

Will Mark write my name on the chalkboard?

No, he will not. *
He will write his name on the chalkboard.

What will you do at noon?

I will have lunch.

What class will you have at 1:00 p.m.?

I will have science.

* will not OR won't

How many pencils do we have?

We have only two.
We have to get another one.

How many brushes do we have?

We have a few.
We have to get some more.

How much paper do we have?

We have only one piece.
We have to get two more pieces.

How many books do we have?

We have only one.
We have to get two more.

How much chalk do we have?

We have only two pieces.
We have to get another piece.

How much paint do we have?

We have a little.
We have to get some more.

We have a lot of brushes.

We have a lot of paint.

	How many do you have?	How many do you want?		How many do you have?	How many do you want?
sausage			orange		
egg			hamburger		
candy bar			hot dog		
cookie			bun		
apple			roll		
banana			sandwich		

	How much do you have?	How much do you want?		How much do you have?	How much do you want?
bowl of cereal			helping of corn		
piece of toast			helping of rice		
bowl of soup			helping of macaroni		
glass of juice			loaf of bread		
glass of milk			piece of cheese		
glass of water			ketchup		
piece of cake			cup of popcorn		
salt			mustard		
pepper			bottle of pop		
helping of meat			piece of candy		

What happened?

What will you do? OR
What are you going to do?

I broke a glass.

I have to pick up the pieces.
Then I will get another glass. OR
Then I am going to get another glass.

What happened?

What will you do? OR
What are you going to do?

I lost my shoes.

I have to find them.
Then I will put them on. OR
Then I am going to put them on.

What happened?

What will you do? OR
What are you going to do?

My dog ripped up this comic book. OR
My dog ripped this comic book up.

I have to pick up the pieces. OR
I have to pick the pieces up.
Then I will buy another comic book. OR
Then I am going to buy another comic book.

What happened?

What will you do? OR
What are you going to do?

I dropped my hamburger.

I have to clean up this mess. OR
I have to clean this mess up.
Then I will buy another hamburger. OR
Then I am going to buy another hamburger.

What happened?

What will you do? OR
What are you going to do?

I spilled my milk on my jeans.

I have to wipe off my jeans. OR
I have to wipe my jeans off.
Then I will get another glass. OR
Then I am going to get another glass.

self test

1

2

3

4

When does school start?

It started fifteen minutes ago.
You are late.

When does school start?

It will start in fifteen minutes. OR
It is going to start in fifteen minutes.
You are early.

When does school start?

It is starting right now.
You are right on time.

When does the bus leave?

BUS TERMINAL

It left ten minutes ago.
You are late.

When does the bus leave?

BUS TERMINAL

It will leave in ten minutes. OR
It is going to leave in ten minutes.
You are early.

When does the bus leave?

BUS TERMINAL

It is leaving right now.
You are right on time.

When does the movie start?

FEATURE PRESENTATION

It is starting right now.
You are right on time.

THE MONSTER IN THE SEA

1:00 p.m.

3:00 p.m.

SECRET AGENT 009

1;15 p.m.

3:15 p.m.

TEXAS COWBOY

1:00 p.m.   3:00 p.m.

FRONTIER JANE

5:00 p.m.

It is 3:30 p.m.

You want to see the movie, "The Monster in the Sea."

You are at the movie theater.

You: When does the movie start?

Ticketseller: It started thirty minutes ago. You are late.

1. It is 12:30 p.m.

   You want to see the movie, "The Monster in the Sea."

   You: _____

   Ticketseller: _____

2. It is 1:15 p.m.

   You want to see the movie, "Secret Agent 009."

   You: _____

   Ticketseller: _____

3. It is 3:10 p.m.

   You want to see the movie, "Texas Cowboy."

   You: _____

   Ticketseller: _____

4. It is 4:00 p.m.

   You want to see the movie, "Texas Cowboy."

   You: _____

   Ticketseller: _____

5. It is 4:15 p.m.

   You want to see the movie, "Frontier Jane."

   You: _____

   Ticketseller: _____

6. It is 5:00 p.m.

   You want to see the movie, "Frontier Jane."

   You: _____

   Ticketseller: _____

7. It is 5:15 p.m.

   You want to see the movie, "Frontier Jane."

   You: _____

   Ticketseller: _____

Ask me what this is. What is that? It is a bar of soap.

Ask me what this is. What is that? It is a box of soap.

Ask me what these are. What are those? They are cartons of milk.

Ask me what these are. What are those? They are cans of soup.

Tell me what this is. It is a glass of milk.

Tell me what this is. It is a piece of paper.

Tell me what these are. They are bottles of pop.

Tell me what these are. They are jars of coffee.

What color is the sky?

It is usually blue.

This sky is not blue.
It is gray.
What color are clouds?

Clouds are usually white.

These clouds are not white.
They are gray.

What color is the sun?

The sun is yellow.

What color is the bark on a tree?

It is usually brown.

What color are tires?

Tires are black.

What color are blades of grass?

They are usually green.

These blades of grass
are not green.

They are brown.

What color are coins?

What color are watches?

What color are keys?

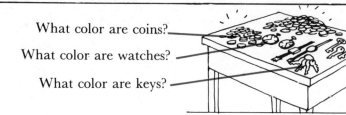

Coins are usually silver.
Some watches are silver.
Some watches are gold.
Some keys are silver.
Some keys are gold.

What color are your eyes?

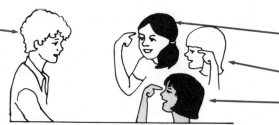

My eyes are brown.

My eyes are blue.

My eyes are black.

What color is your hair?

My hair is blond.

My hair is black.

My hair is red.

My hair is brown.

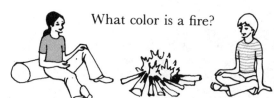

What color is a fire?

A fire is red.

unit twelve

PRONUNCIATION

Theophilus, the thistle sifter,
While sifting a sifter full of
thistles,
Thrust three thousand thistles
Through the thickness of his
thumb.

Where are you?

I am on the teacher's desk.
OR I am on top of the teacher's desk.

I am behind the teacher's desk.

I am next to the teacher's desk.

I am under the teacher's desk.

I am in front of the teacher's desk.

We are near the teacher's desk.

We are in the doorway.
He is in a corner.

We are far from the teacher's desk.

Where are they?

They are on a plane. OR
They are on an airplane.

They are on a bus.

They are on a train.

They are in a car. OR
They are in an automobile.

They are in a truck.

They are on a motorcycle.

They are on a horse.

They are on a bicycle.

They are in a boat.

Is he on a bicycle or on a motorcycle?

He is on a motorcycle.

Are they on a plane or on a train?

They are on a plane.

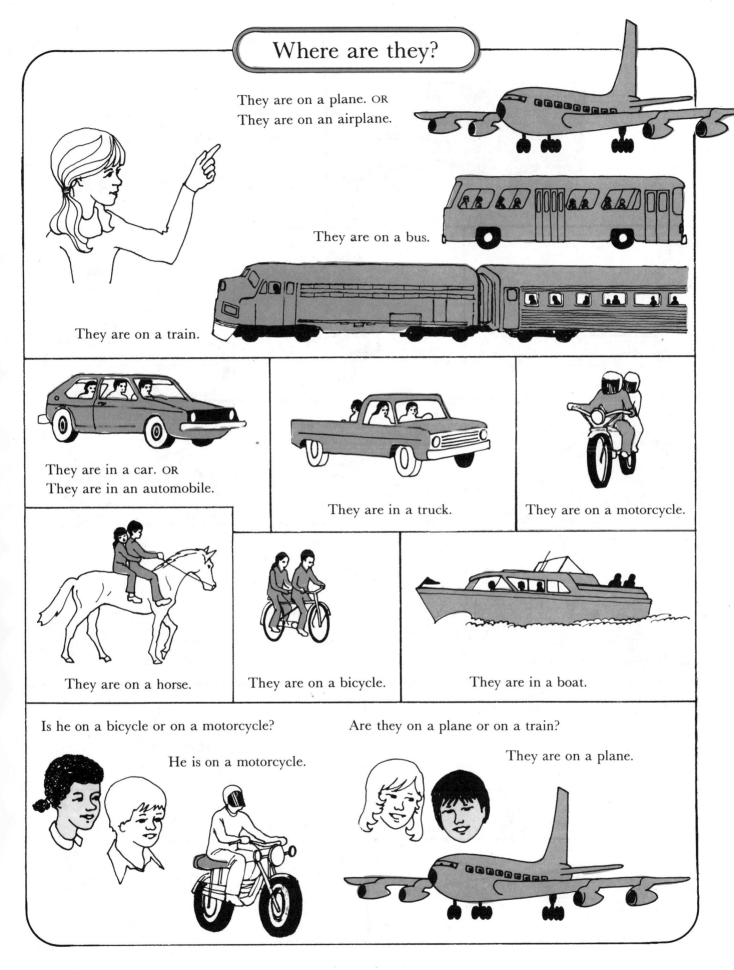

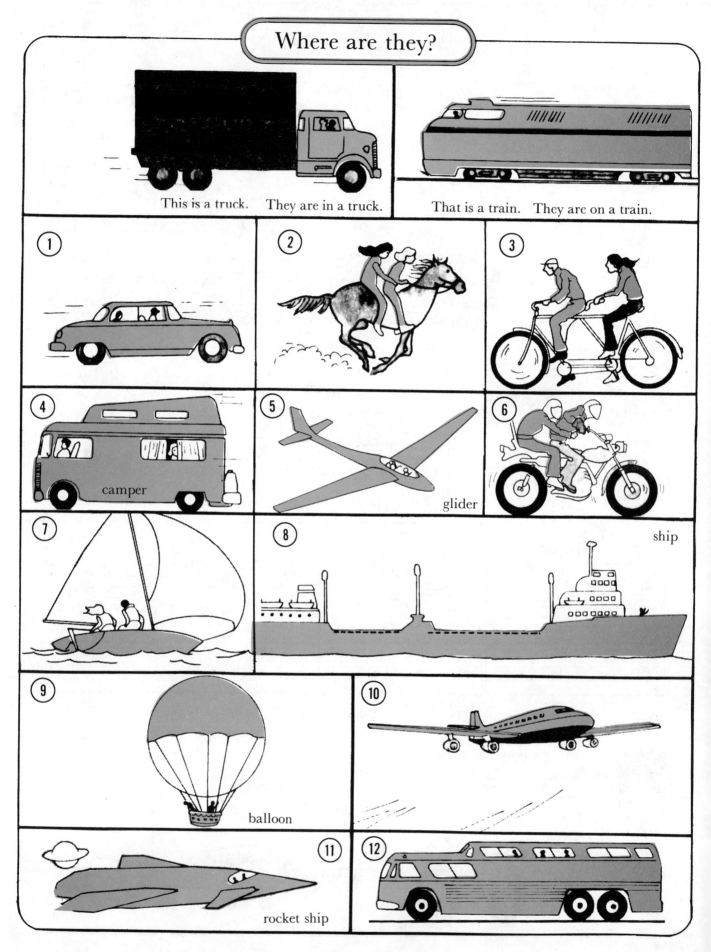

Where are they?

This is a truck. They are in a truck.

That is a train. They are on a train.

glider

ship

camper

balloon

rocket ship

I do not have an eraser.
Please lend me your eraser. OR
Please lend your eraser to me.

All right.

He lent me his eraser. OR
He lent his eraser to me.

I do not have any paper.
Please give me a piece.

All right.

She gave me a piece. OR
She gave a piece to me.

I cannot see your faces.
Please show me your faces.

All right.

They showed me their faces. OR
They showed their faces to me.

I have to have my eraser.
Please give me back my eraser. OR
Please give my eraser back to me.

All right.

She gave me back my eraser. OR
She gave my eraser back to me.

Get them some towels. OR
Get some towels for them.

We got them some towels. OR
We got some towels for them.

Please make us some hot chocolate. OR
Please make some hot chocolate for us.

They made us some hot chocolate. OR
They made some hot chocolate for us.

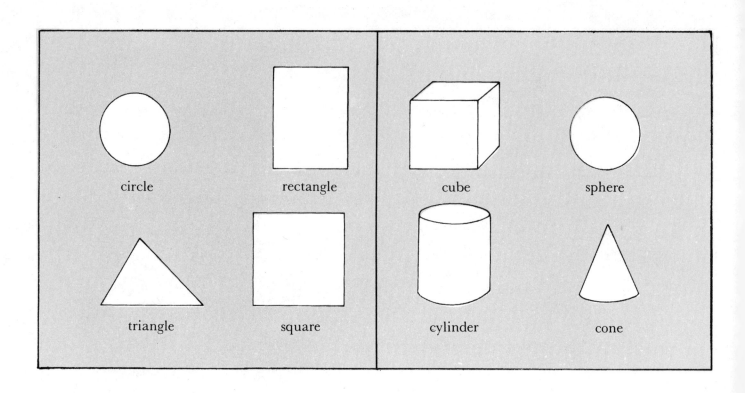

circle

rectangle

cube

sphere

triangle

square

cylinder

cone

How do they look?

He looks sad.

She looks happy.

They look angry.

He looks sick.

She looks tired.

They look hot.

She looks cold.

He looks thirsty.

They look hungry.

They look nice.

They look scared.

You look sad.  I am.
I lost my books.

You look happy.  I am.
I have a new bicycle.

You look angry. I am.
My younger brother ripped up my comic books.

You look sick.  I am.
I had ten hot dogs and five bottles of pop.

You look hot. I am.
This sweater is too heavy. I have to take it off.

You look cold. We are.
Please close the door.

You look tired.

We are.
We washed six cars.

You look thirsty.

We are.
We want to drink some water.

You look hungry.

I am. There is not any food here.

You look scared.

I am. Look at this. It is a monster's footprint.

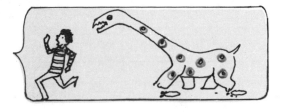

You look nice.

Thank you.
Our parents gave us new clothes.

How do they feel?

He feels sick.

They feel angry.

She feels good.

Why do you feel angry?	I feel angry because you lost my ring.
Why do you feel hungry?	I feel hungry because I did not have any breakfast.
Why do you feel good?	I feel good because I came to school by plane.
Why do you feel sad?	I feel sad because I cannot see my family.

REGULAR VERBS

A

I		II		III	
clear	cleared	ask	asked	point	pointed
comb		brush		sift	
crawl		dress		start	
fill		drop		toot	
happen		help		want	
listen		jump			
open		kick			
roll		look			
seem		mix			
show		pick			
spill		pinch			
stay		punch			
		reach			
		talk			
		thank			
		toss			
		touch			
		walk			
		wash			
		watch			

B

I		II		III	
grab	grabbed	rip	ripped		
stir		stop			

C

I		II		III	
close	closed	like	liked	violate	violated
measure		wipe			
move					
please					
save					
tickle					
use					

D

I			
carry	carried		
dry			
fry			

Examples

I   CLEAR   the table *every day*.
I *am* CLEAR*ing* the table *now*.
I   CLEAR*ed*   the table *yesterday*.

IRREGULAR VERBS

1.

len*d*	len*t*
ma*k*e	ma*d*e

2.

br*ing*	br*ought*
bu*y*	b*ought*
ca*tch*	c*aught*
f*ee*l	f*e*lt
h*ear*	h*eard*
l*eave*	l*e*ft
l*ose*	l*ost*
sa*y*	s*aid*
sl*eep*	sl*e*pt
t*eac*h	t*aught*
t*ell*	t*old*

3.

hit	hit
let	let
put	put

4.

find	found
get	got
hold	held
lead	led
meet	met
read	read
sit	sat
stand	stood

5.

6.

break	broke
drive	drove
fall	fell
fly	flew
give	gave
grow	grew
ride	rode
see	saw
take	took
wake	woke
wear	wore
write	wrote

7.

come	came
go	went
run	ran
sing	sang

BE

I	am	walking.			
We	are	walking.	He	is	walking.
You	are	walking.	She	is	walking.
They	are	walking.	It	is	walking.

DO

Do	I	have ears?			
Do	we	have ears?	Does	he	have ears?
Do	you	have ears?	Does	she	have ears?
Do	they	have ears?	Does	it	have ears?

HAVE

I	have	ears.			
We	have	ears.	He	has	ears.
You	have	ears.	She	has	ears.
They	have	ears.	It	has	ears.

EAT

I	eat	every day.			
We	eat	every day.	He	eats	every day.
You	eat	every day.	She	eats	every day.
They	eat	every day.	It	eats	every day.

This chart is based upon the classification of verbs given in:
Quirk, Randolph; Greenbaum, Sidney; Leech, Geoffrey; Svartik, Jan. *A Grammar of Contemporary English*, pp. 106-121.
London, Longman Group Ltd., 1972.

WORD LIST

a *8*
acrylic *68*
after *32*
afternoon *33*
agent *109*
ago *108*
airplane *87*
all *117*
along *47*
always *41*
am *8*
a.m. *32*
amounts *99*
an *37*
and *18*
angry *121*
another *103*
any *26*
apple *38*
apples *38*
are *6*
arms *14*
around *101*
art *72*
as *60*
ask *110*
assignment *79*
at *36*
ate *75*
attack *90*
aunts *51*
automobile *115*
avenue *47*
babies *91*
baby *51*
back *90*
backwards *64*
bad *83*
ball *10*
balloon *116*
banana *38*
bananas *38*
bar *110*
bark *85*
baseball *45*
basketball *45*
bathroom *95*
batter *70*
be *62*
because *124*
bed *23*
beef *37*
before *71*
begin *90*
behind *114*
belt *16*
better *70*
bicycle *48*
big *58*
bigger *58*
biggest *59*
bird *66*
birds *62*
birthday *43*

bit *70*
bitter *70*
black *111*
blade *85*
blades *111*
block *47*
blocks *47*
blond *112*
blouse *16*
blue *111*
boat *49*
body *14*
book *8*
bookcase *86*
books *22*
bottle *39*
bottles *39*
bottom *56*
bought *70*
bouncing *10*
bowl *39*
bowls *39*
box *9*
boy *21*
boys *25*
branches *85*
bread *38*
breakfast *18*
brick *84*
bring *118*
broke *106*
brother *51*
brothers *51*
brought *118*
brown *111*
brush *34*
brushes *25*
brushing *18*
bumpy *82*
bun *104*
bus *48*
bush *57*
but *70*
butter *70*
buy *106*
by *48*
cake *38*
calendar *30*
calendars *24*
came *74*
camper *116*
can *42*
candy *38*
candy bar *104*
canner *60*
cannot *66*
cans *60*
canvas *86*
car *48*
cardboard *84*
carried *76*
carrot *37*
carry *66*
carrying *76*

cars *62*
cartons *110*
cat *92*
catch *42*
catching *10*
cats *91*
ceiling *76*
centimeters *55*
cereal *38*
chair *22*
chairs *25*
chalk *25*
chalkboard *66*
chalkboards *24*
cheese *105*
chest *14*
chicken *37*
chickens *37*
child *75*
chocolate *119*
circle *120*
class *71*
clean *83*
clear *34*
cleared *76*
clearing *18*
clocks *24*
close *65*
closed *74*
closet *23*
closing *8*
cloth *68*
clothes *15*
cloud *61*
clouds *62*
coat *16*
coats *72*
coffee *110*
coins *112*
color *111*
cold *82*
comb *34*
combed *77*
combing *18*
come *37*
comic *106*
coming *48*
concert *45*
concrete *86*
cone *120*
cookie *38*
cookies *38*
corn *37*
corner *114*
corners *24*
cousins *51*
cow *37*
cowboy *109*
cows *37*
crab *42*
crack *90*
crawl *66*
crib *42*
crooked *91*

cross *47*
cube *84*
cup *105*
cylinder *120*
dark *83*
date *43*
day *43*
decks *70*
desk *21*
desks *19*
detective *74*
did *76*
different *99*
dirty *83*
disappeared *75*
do *34*
does *35*
dog *62*
doghouse *87*
dogs *91*
doing *6*
door *8*
doors *26*
doorway *88*
down *7*
drawer *95*
dress *16*
dresses *23*
drink *65*
drive *88*
dropped *106*
drugstore *44*
dry *82*
ducks *70*
dull *83*
early *108*
ears *14*
east *47*
eat *34*
eating *18*
eats *35*
egg *37*
eggs *37*
eight *24*
eighteen *25*
eighth *43*
eighty *31*
eleven *25*
English language *72*
eraser *117*
erasers *30*
evening *33*
every *34*
everyone *90*
eyes *14*
face *34*
faces *18*
falling *11*
family *51*
far *114*
faster *90*
fat *91*
father *51*
fatter *92*

feel *13*
feeling *42*
feels *82*
feet *13*
felt *82*
fence *56*
few *29*
fifteen *25*
fifth *43*
fifty *31*
filling *42*
find *75*
finger *98*
fingers *14*
finish *69*
fire *84*
first *43*
fish *37*
five *24*
floor *21*
flower *85*
flowers *62*
flute *81*
fly *66*
food *123*
foot *57*
footprint *75*
for *41*
forty *31*
foster parents *53*
found *75*
four *24*
fourteen *25*
fourth *43*
Friday *43*
frigid *13*
from *37*
front *90*
frontier *109*
fry *42*
full *113*
game *45*
gas *44*
gave *117*
get *47*
getting *8*
girl *48*
girls *24*
give *117*
glass *37*
glasses *21*
glider *116*
go *35*
goes *44*
going *44*
gold *112*
good *32*
got *77*
grabbed *74*
grabbing *74*
grandfather *54*
grandfathers *51*
grandmothers *51*
grandparents *53*

shed 60
sheep 37
shelf 56
shelves 25
shiny 83
ship 116
shirt 13
shirts 17
shoe 16
shoes 15
short 13
should 60
shoulders 14
show 117
showed 117
sick 121
sifter 113
sifting 113
sign 92
silver 112
sing 66
sister 51
sisters 51
sit 65
sitting 7
six 24
sixteen 25
sixth 43
sixty 31
size 59
skirt 16
sky 61
sleep 60
sleeping 18
slice 39
slices 39
slipper 84
small 92
smell 83
smelled 83
smells 83
smooth 82
snack 41
snake 66
so 70
soap 110
soccer 45
social studies 72
socks 15
soft 82
soil 85
some 40
sometimes 41
song 90
songs 66
sorry 23
soup 38
south 47
space 88
Spanish language 72

sphere 116
spilled 106
spinach 37
square 120
squares 69
stairs 86
stand 95
standing 6
star 61
start 69
started 108
starting 108
station 44
stay 97
steer 37
steers 37
stem 85
stepfather 53
stereo 80
stir 42
stockings 15
stone 82
stones 85
stop 102
store 44
story 74
straight 91
street 47
student 27
students 25
sun 61
Sunday 43
supermarket 44
supper 35
sweater 16
swim 66
swimming 45
table 18
take 65
taking 18
talk 95
tall 55
taller 55
tallest 55
taxi 48
teach 81
teacher 26
teachers 24
teeth 18
telephone 87
tell 110
ten 24
tenth 43
test 12
than 54
thank 123
that 16
the 9
theater 47
their 17

them 73
then 47
there 26
these 14
they 15
thick 57
thicker 57
thickness 59
thin 91
things 98
third 43
thirsty 121
thirteen 25
thirteenth 43
thirtieth 43
thirty 31
this 14
thistle 113
thistles 113
those 16
thousand 31
three 20
through 88
throwing 10
thrust 113
thumb 98
Thursday 43
ticketseller 109
tickle 75
tickled 75
tile 86
time 32
tire 84
tired 121
tires 84
to 32
toast 38
today 43
toes 14
tomato 37
tomorrow 43
tongue 82
too 88
took 77
toot 81
tooted 81
tooters 81
top 56
toss 42
touch 66
touched 76
touching 76
towel 91
towels 119
track 90
train 48
tree 55
triangle 120
tried 81
truck 48

trunk 85
Tuesday 43
turn 46
turning 46
tutor 81
TV 35
twelve 25
twentieth 43
twenty 25
twin 51
two 13
uncles 51
under 21
underwear 16
unit 5
up 6
upside down 64
us 119
use 88
usually 41
vegetables 37
vine 13
vinyl 68
violates 13
waist 14
wake 34
wakes 35
waking 18
walk 47
walked 76
walking 6
walks 47
wall 24
walls 30
want 38
wants 96
was 43
wash 34
washed 76
washing 18
wastebaskets 25
watch 35
watches 35
water 38
way 90
we 6
wear 88
Wednesday 43
week 43
weekdays 43
weekend 43
weigh 99
went 77
west 47
wet 82
what 6
wheels 90
when 36
where 21
which 55

while 113
white 111
who 81
whose 15
why 124
wide 57
wider 57
widest 58
width 59
will 70
window 8
windows 26
wipe 106
won't 101
wood 68
wooden 86
would 38
wristwatch 68
write 95
wrong 64
year 43
years 54
yellow 111
yes 6
yesterday 43
you 6
young 81
younger 51
youngest 54
your 15
zipper 84